Carnival Towel

CREATIONS

40 DESIGNS

❩Carnival.
Towel
CREATIONS

Dear "Fun Ship"® Guest.

Carnival's towel animals are a very popular and talked about feature aboard the "Fun Ships"®.

In fact over the years we have received literally hundreds of requests from guests wanting to know how they can re-create these fun creatures. That deer you admired so much, or the rabbit and swan that are part of your holiday album can now be brought back to life.

That is why we have decided to publish this book, "Towel Creations" which offers a visit to the Carnival Towel Animal Farm and easy step-by-step instructions for creating dozens of different animals.

You will notice that many of the instructional images from the book were taken in Bangkok, Thailand, home to the world's most experienced and creative towel folders.

We hope you enjoy this new book and the magic it brings!

See you soon,
Your Hotel Team

SECOND EDITION. Copyright © 2004 Navigate Express CO.,LTD.

Carnival® is a registered trademark of Carnival Cruise Lines
3655 N.W. 87th Avenue, Miami, Florida 33178-2428
Executive office: 800 555 5555
www.carnival.com

Contents

Towel Creations

Things you need before starting

Advice: 100 % cotton towel

Use a "washed" towel because it is easier to shape the animal.

Size:			
	Large towel	30 x 50	inches (or similar)
	Medium towel	17 x 28	inches (or similar)
	Washcloth	12 x 12	inches (or similar)

Decorations:

Advice: Use colored or plain paper for eyes, nose and whiskers as it will adhere to the fabric easily.

Make the animals look cuter by adding sunglasses or ribbon.

Useful guidelines and tricks to make them look even more alive.

- After finishing your animal towel, place it on a blanket, sheet or another towel. It will protect it from slipping and maintain its shape.
- The Main Body "A" and "B" does not need to be tight except for Main Body "C".
- For stability use safety pins behind the head or body.

Making Main Body

Main Body **A**

Prepare a large towel

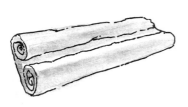

Step1 : Roll tightly each side widthwise to the center.

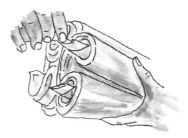

Step 2: Fold the towel in half with both back sides joining to make four rolls then pull the towel corner out of each roll.

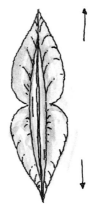

Step 3: Each hand holds the top and bottom towel corners then pull apart to form the Main Body.

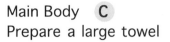

Main Body B
Prepare a large towel

Main Body C
Prepare a large towel

Step 1 : Have a second person hold or hang the center of the towel on a hook.

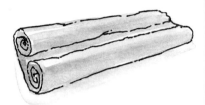

Step 1 : Roll tightly each side widthwise to the center.

Step 2 : Fold the towel in half with both back sides joining to make four rolls then pull the towel corner out of each roll.

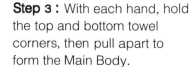

Step 3 : With each hand, hold the top and bottom towel corners, then pull apart to form the Main Body.

Step 4 : Bring back legs around the body to the front and bend front legs upwards to reach sitting position.

Step 2 : Roll tightly both sides to the center.

7

Bat

Body : Refer to Main Body **A** .
Place it upside down and pull the top layer back to cover the legs.

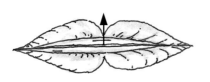

Head : Prepare a washcloth.

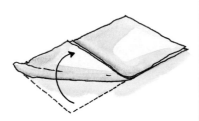

Step 1 : Fold it in half and fold two corners below to the center to form a triangle.

Step 2 : Roll both triangles into the middle then turn back and pull the center down.

Step 3 : Pull the forehead down and shape the ears. Place it on the body.

Bulldog

Body : Refer to Main Body **A**

Head : Prepare medium towel and fold lengthwise.

Step 1 : Fold it in half.

Step 2 : Pull two bottom corners to the center to form a triangle.

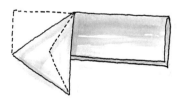

Step 3 : Tuck the pointed sides in.

Step 4 : Roll both sides into the middle and hold it tightly and shape it as a "Bulldog". Place it on the body.

Bunny

Body : Refer to Main Body **A** but pull a bit longer.

Head : Prepare medium towel and fold widthwise.

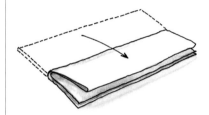

Step 1 : Fold it in half and fold it over again.

Step 2 : Pull two corners down to the center to form a triangle.

Step 3 : Tuck the pointed side in and roll both sides into the center.

Step 4 : Pull up the two corners to shape the ears. Pull the forehead down and place it on the body.

Cobra

Body : Prepare large towel.

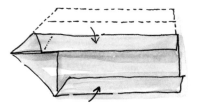

Step 1 : Fold two inches widthwise.

Step 2 : Fold two upper corners to the center to form triangles. Roll lengthwise over until the end.

Step 3 : Twist it over until the end and knot it to shape as a "Cobra".

Towel Creations

Body : Refer to Main Body Ⓐ

Head : Prepare medium towel and fold widthwise.

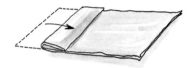

Step 1 : Fold it in half and then fold the bottom in two inches.

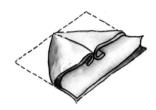

Step 2 : Fold two corners down to the center to form a triangle.

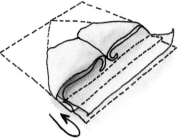

Step 3 : Tuck the pointed side in and fold the one below in half.

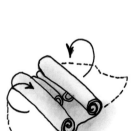

Step 4 : Roll tightly both sides to the center.

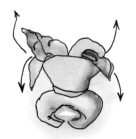

Step 5 : Slightly pull the forehead down, shape the ears and horns. Place it on the body.

Crocodile

Body : Refer to Main Body **B**

Tail : Prepare a Main Body **C** using a medium towel, and place it in between the body.

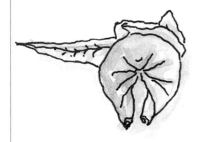

Head : Prepare medium towel and fold widthwise.

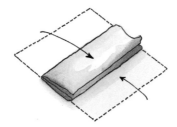

Step 1 : Make three folds.

Step 2 : Fold two sides to the center to form a triangle then fold two corners of triangle up.

Step 3 : Hold it tightly and place it in the center of the Main Body. Press and turn it upside down to shape a "Crocodile".

Deer

Body : Refer to Main Body Ⓐ

Head : Prepare medium towel and fold lengthwise.

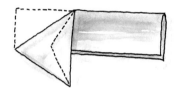

Step 1 : Fold it in half and fold two corners to the center to form a triangle.

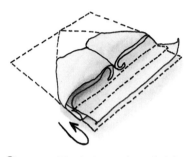

Step 2 : Tuck the pointed side in and fold the one below in half.

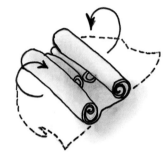

Step 3 : Roll tightly both sides to the center.

Step 4 : Hold it tightly and pull the forehead down. Shape the ears and the horns. Place it on the body.

Dinosaur

Body : Refer to Main Body B

Tail : Use a medium towel to prepare the Main Body C . Put it in between the body.

Head : Prepare medium towel.

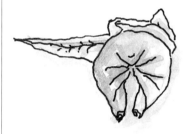

Step 1 : Use the medium towel to prepare the Main Body C . Put it in between the Main Body B and place it in the sitting position.

Step 2 : Bend the head and shape the pointed side as a Dinosaur face.

Donkey

Body : Refer to Main Body **B**

Head : Prepare medium towel and fold lengthwise.

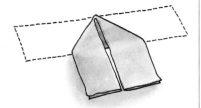

Step 1 : Fold it in half and fold two sides to the center to form a triangle.

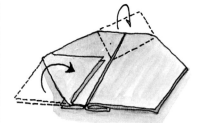

Step 2 : Tuck the pointed side in and fold both corners to the center to form a triangle.

Step 3 : Roll both sides to the center.

Step 4 : Hold it tightly and pull the forehead down. Shape the mouth and ears. Place it on the body.

Frog

Body : Refer to Main Body **B**

Head : Prepare medium towel and fold widthwise.

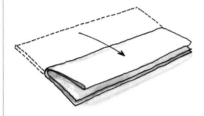

Step 1 : Fold it in half and fold it over again.

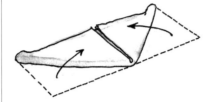

Step 2 : Fold both edges into the center to form a triangle.

Step 3 : Fold the triangle backwards and fold the two pointed edges in half. Shape the face as a smiling frog. Place it in the body.

Hanging Monkey

Body : Refer to Main Body **A** and hold 2 legs in each hand then pull apart to make it longer and hang it up.

Head : Prepare medium towel
and fold widthwise.

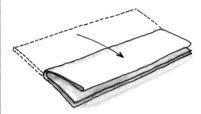

Step 1 : Fold it in half and fold it over again.

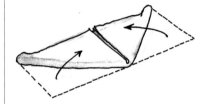

Step 2 : Fold both edges into the center to form a triangle.

Step 3 : Fold the triangle backwards and fold the two pointed edges in half. Shape the face as a monkey. Place it in the body.

Horse

Body : Refer to Main Body **B**

Tail : Prepare a washcloth then roll from the top corner to the end and put it in the body. Fold, press and turn it in the sitting position.

Head : Prepare medium towel and fold widthwise.	**Step 1 :** Fold it in half and fold the open sides two inches in.	**Step 2 :** Fold both corners to the center to form a triangle.

Step 3 : Tuck the pointed side in and fold the bottom up.

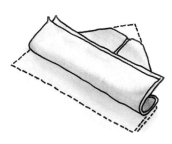

Step 4 : Make a small triangle in both corners and roll both sides tightly to the center.

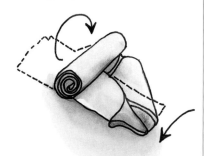

Step 5 : Pull the forehead down and adjust the mouth. Place it on the body.

Iguana

Body : Refer to Main Body **B**

Tail : Use the medium towel to prepare the Main Body **C** . Put it in between the body.

Head : Prepare medium towel and fold widthwise.

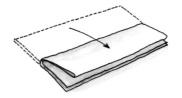

Step 1 : Fold it in half and fold it over again.

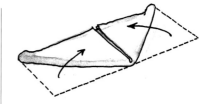

Step 2 : Fold two sides into the center to form a triangle.

Step 3 : Turn back and fold about one inch backwards.

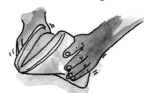

Step 4 : Pull two ends together and shape the open side as a mouth. Place it on the body.

Step 5 : Hold it tightly and place it in the center of the Main Body. Press and turn it upside down to shape an "Iguana".

Jumbo

Body : Refer to Main Body Ⓐ

Head : Prepare medium towel.

Step 1 : Fold it in half.

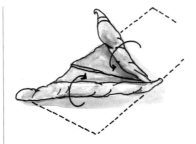

Step 2 : Roll both sides to the center.

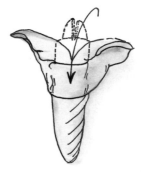

Step 3 : Pull the center out as the ears and roll the long end upward as a trunk and then place it on the body.

Towel Creations

Kitty

Body : Refer to Main Body B

Tail : Prepare a washcloth and roll it until the end. Put it in between the body then fold, press, turn and place it in a sitting position.

Head : Prepare medium towel and fold lengthwise.

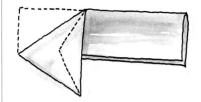

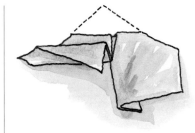

Step 1 : Fold it in half and fold two sides to the center to form a triangle.

Step 2 ; Tuck the pointed shape in and fold the end up then fold back in half.

Step 3 : Roll both sides tightly into the middle.

Step 4 : Pull out the nose and put some inside then fold the forehead a little down and place it on the body.

Towel Creations

Lion

Body : Refer to Main Body (B)

Tail : Prepare a washcloth then roll from the top corner to the end and put it in between the body.

Head : Prepare medium towel and fold widthwise.

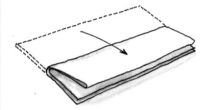

Step 1 : Fold it in half and fold it over again.

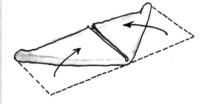

Step 2 : Fold two corners to the center to form a triangle.

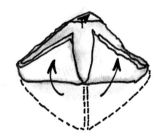

Step 3 : Turn it and fold it in half and put it in between the two front legs. Hold the body and place it in a sitting position.

Towel Creations

Little Duck

Body : Prepare large towel.

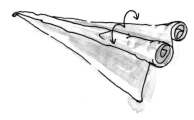

Step 1 : Have a second person hold or hang the center of the towel on a hook.

Step 2 : Roll tightly both sides to the center.

Step 3 : Bend half of it down in a sitting position to form a "Duck".

Lizard

Body : Refer to Main Body **B**

Tail : Prepare medium towel then refer to Main Body **C** and put it in between the body.

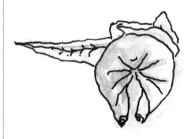

Head : Prepare medium towel and fold widthwise.

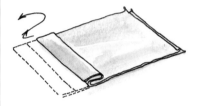

Step 1 : Fold it in half and fold one side in two inches and fold it back in half again.

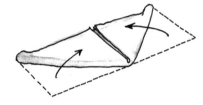

Step 2 : Fold two corners in to form a triangle and roll both sides into the middle.

Step 3 : Hold it tightly and put it in between the front legs. Fold, press and turn the shape to form a "Lizard".

Lobster

Body: Refer to Main Body C

Tail : Prepare medium towel.

Step 1 : Refer to Main Body C , turn two arms around and squeeze them to make the claws.

Step 2 : Spread the medium towel on top of the body.

Step 3 : Fold into two inch strips, so that each strip overlaps. Tuck both sides underneath.

Head : Prepare medium towel and fold widthwise.

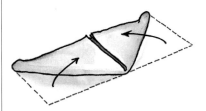

Step 1 : Make three folds and fold two corners to the center to form a triangle.

Step 2 : Fold it in half and place it on the body and shape to form a "Lobster".

Lying Monkey

Body : Refer to Main Body Ⓐ
Pull apart to make the body longer, and place it in a lying position.

Head : Prepare medium towel and fold lengthwise.

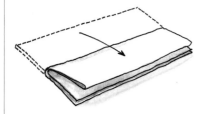

Step 1 : Fold it in half and fold it over again.

Step 2 : Roll from the right to the left.

Hat : Prepare a washcloth.

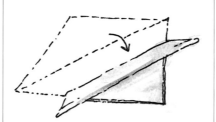

Step 1 : Fold it in half to form a triangle and fold about one inch down.

Step 2 : Tie it around the head and place it on the body.

Lying Pig

Body : Refer to Main Body **A** in lying position.

Head : Prepare medium towel and fold lengthwise.

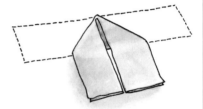

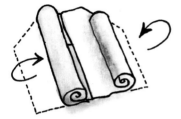

Step 1 : Fold it in half and fold two corners to the center to form a triangle.

Step 2 : Tuck the pointed shape in.

Step 3 : Roll tightly both sides into the middle then pull the forehead down a bit. Adjust the nose and mouth then place it on the body.

Towel Creations

Mouse

Tail :   Prepare medium towel. Roll from the top corner to the end and put it in the body.

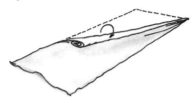

Body : Prepare large towel.

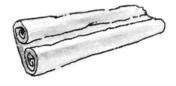

Step 1 : Roll both sides to the center, making one bigger than the other.

Step 2 : Fold it in half to make four rolls and place it in a lying position.

Head : Prepare medium towel.

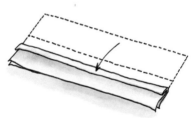

Step 1 : Fold it in half and fold two inches from the bottom up.

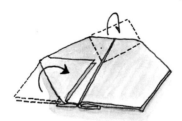

Step 3 : Tuck the pointed shape in and fold both corners to the center to form a triangle.

Step 2 : Hold the center bottom and fold two sides to the center to form a triangle.

Step 4 : Roll both sides to the center and hold in tightly. Roll two rolls as the ears and place it on the body.

Parrot

Body : Refer to Main Body **B**

Tail : Prepare medium towel then fold it in half and fold again three times then put it in between the body.

Head : Prepare medium towel and fold widthwise.

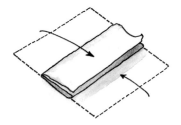

Step 1 : Make three folds.

Step 2 : Fold it in half and fold downward in half again.

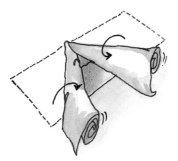

Step 3 : Roll two sides to the center to form a triangle. Hold it in tightly and pull the pointed shape as a beak. Place it on the body and fold, press and turn, then place it in a sitting position.

Peacock

Body : Refer to Main Body **B**

Tail : Prepare medium towel then fold about one inch over and over and put it in between the body.

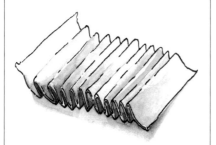

Head : Prepare medium towel.

Step 1 : Roll from the top of both sides to the center and put it in the body.

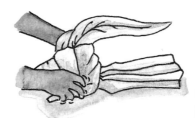

Step 3 : Put two hands beside the body and make a curving head.

Step 2 : Fold, press and turn then place it in a sitting position.

Piggy

Body : Refer to Main Body **A** and put it in a sitting position.

Head : Prepare medium towel and fold widthwise.

Step 1 : Fold it in half and fold one inch down.

Step 2 : Fold two corners to the center in triangle.

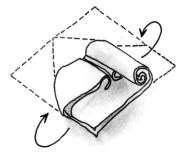

Step 3 : Tuck the pointed end in and roll both sides into the middle.

Step 4 : Pull the forehead a bit down to make the ears. Adjust the nose and mouth then place it on the body.

Polar Bear

Body : Refer to Main Body **B**

Head : Prepare medium towel and fold widthwise.

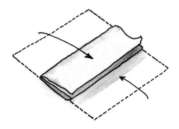

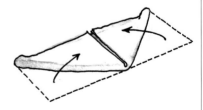

Step 1 : Make three folds and fold two sides to the center to form a triangle and roll both sides into the middle.

Step 2 : Open the back up and pull two triangles up as the ears.

Step 3 : Hold the two ends behind it tightly and place it in between the body. Fold, press and turn, then place in a sitting position.

Puppy

Body : Refer to Main Body B

Tail : Prepare a washcloth. Roll from the top corner to the end and put it in the body. Fold, press and turn it in a sitting position.

Head : Prepare medium towel and fold lengthwise.

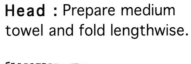

Step 1 : Fold it in half and fold two sides to the center in to form a triangle.

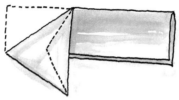

Step 2 : Tuck the pointed shape in and roll both sides into the middle. Pull the ears down and place it on the body.

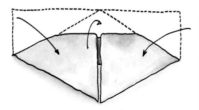

Towel Creations

Rabbit

Body : Refer to Main Body (A)

Head : Prepare medium towel.

Step 1 : Have a second person hold or hang the center of the towel on a hook.

Step 2 : Roll tightly both sides to the center.

Step 3 : Turn the long ended sides around and tuck it inside. Shape the ears. Place it on the body.

Towel Creations

Scorpion

Body : Prepare large towel.

Refer to Main Body C
Turn and squeeze to form
the shape of the claws.

Head : Prepare medium
towel and fold lengthwise.

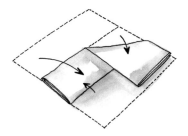

Step 1 : Make three folds and
fold two sides to the center to
form a triangle.

Step 3 : Shape the head and tail
as a "Scorpion".

Step 2 : Put it over the body
and tuck two ends underneath.

65

Seahorse

Body : Prepare large towel.

Step1 : Have a second person hold or hang the center of the towel on a hook.

Step 2 : Roll tightly both sides to the center.

Step 3 : Hold two rolls tightly and tie the ends together and bend the body to shape "Seahorse".

Seal

Body : Prepare large towel and fold widthwise.

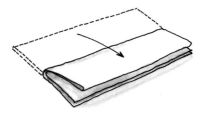

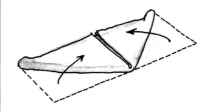

Step 1 : Fold it in half and fold it over again.

Step 2 : Fold two upper corners into the middle to form a triangle.

Step 3 : Fold the triangle in half and put it in a standing position. With two triangles down as legs, hold the top triangle as a head. Shape to form a "Seal".

Sitting Elephant

Body : Prepare large towel.

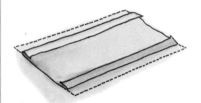

Step 1 : Fold lengthwise two inches of the top and the bottom.

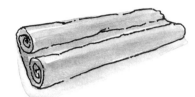

Step 2 : Roll widthwise both sides in to the center.

Step 3 : Fold in half to make four legs. Place it in a sitting position.

Head : Prepare medium towel and fold widthwise.

Step 1 : Hang the center of the towel on a hook. Roll tightly both sides towards the center.

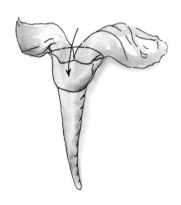

Step 2 : Pull the forehead down and shape the ears.

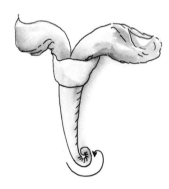

Step 3 : Shape the nose and place it on the body.

Sitting Monkey

Body : Refer to Main Body B

Tail : Prepare a wash-cloth and roll it from one corner until the end. Place it in between the body. Fold, press and turn and put it in a sitting position.

Head : Prepare medium towel and fold lengthwise. Have a washcloth ready.

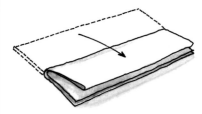

Step 1 : Fold it in half and fold it over again.

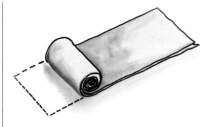

Step 2 : Roll from the right to the left.

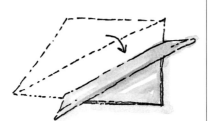

Step 3 : Fold the washcloth in half to form a triangle. Fold about one inch down then tie it around the head and place it on the body.

Snail

Body : Prepare large towel.

Step 1 : Hook to a support and pull to the center. Tightly roll both sides of the towel to the center.

Step 2 : Roll the two long tails upwards.

Step 3 : Tie both ends and shape it as a "Snail".

Snoozing Dog

Body : Refer to Main Body (A)

Head : Prepare medium towel and fold lengthwise.

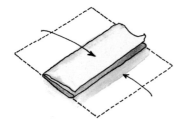

Step 1 : Make three folds.

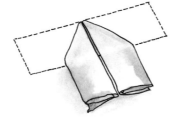

Step 2 : Fold two sides to the center to form a triangle.

Step 3 : Fold it in half and leave the ears. Adjust the head, place it on the body.

Standing Elephant

Body : Prepare large towel.

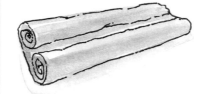

Step 1 : Fold the top and bottom two inches in.

Step 2 : Roll the right and the left towards the center.

Step 3 : Fold in half to make four rolls then place in a standing position.

Head : Prepare medium towel.

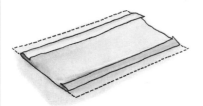

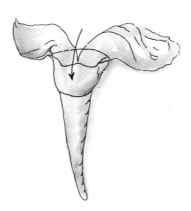

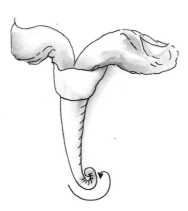

Step 1 : Hook the center and roll both sides towards the middle.

Step 2 : Pull the lower right and left corners down to form ears.

Step 3 : Hold in tightly and roll the long end backward as a trunk. Place it on the body and a "Standing Elephant" is completed.

Stingray

Body : Refer to Main Body **A** .

Place it upside down and pull the top layer back to cover the legs.

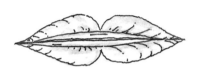

Tail : Prepare medium towel. Roll from the top corner to the end and put it in the body.

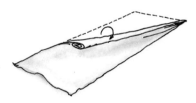

Towel Creations

Body : Refer to Main Body (C) then fold about 3/4 backwards and set the point up as a mouth.

Tail : Prepare medium towel.

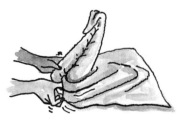

Step 1 : Spread medium towel over the bottom body. Tuck two corners in the front of the body.

Step 2 : Pick the center up and put the rest underneath to make it stand.

Towel Creations

Turtle

Body : Refer to Main Body ⓑ

Head : Prepare medium towel and fold widthwise.

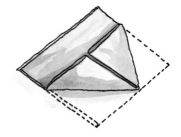

Step 1 : Fold it in half and fold two corners in to form a triangle.

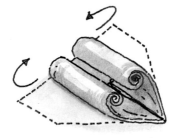

Step 2 : Roll both sides to the center.

Step 3 : Hold it tightly and place it in the center of the Main Body.

Step 4 : Fold, press and turn it upside down to shape a "Turtle".

Worm

Body : Prepare large towel.

Step 1 : Fold towel in half, then fold one side in about two inches. Fold two sides to the center to form a triangle.

Step 2 : Fold so that two inches overlap each other.

Step 3 : Roll and adjust it, then pull the head up.

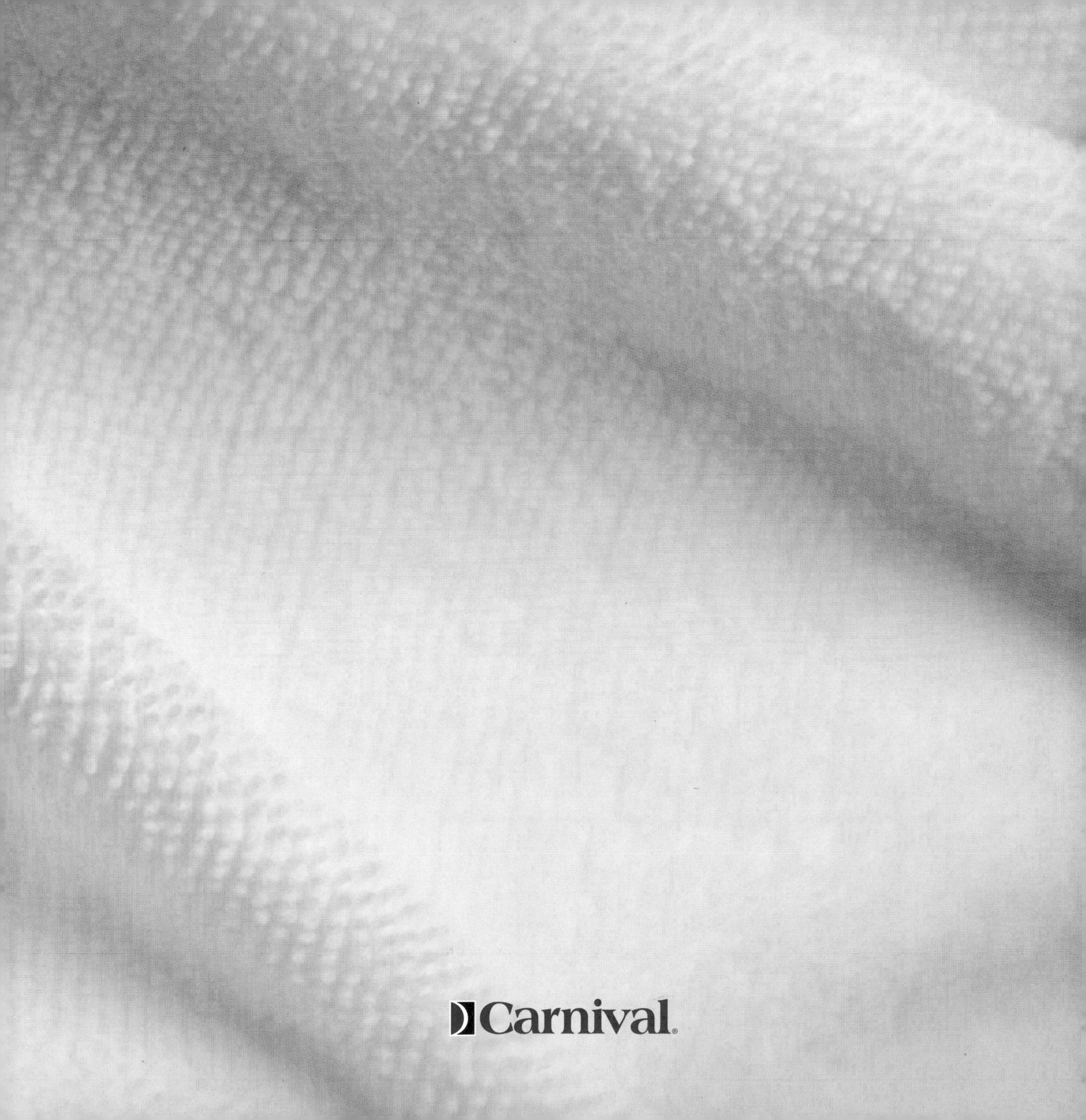
Carnival